BE FREE FROM

Spirit Spouses

(Marine Spirits)

BY

ZITA GRANT

MW00463497

COPYRIGHT

No part of this book may be reproduced, or stored in a retrieval system, or transmitted in any form or by any means, electronic, mechanical, photocopying, recording, or otherwise, without the express written permission of the publisher.

Text copyright © 2017 by Zita Grant

Printed in the United States of America

ISBN 978-1945491115

All rights reserved.

Published by 2 Tigers LLC

Cover design by 2 Tigers LLC

The first edition

ACKNOWLEDGMENTS

Thank you, Heavenly Father, for answering my prayers regarding many things covered in this book. Also, I give you all the glory, honor, and praise as repeatedly your Word has never failed those that choose to believe in your Son, Jesus Christ.

Special thanks to the people who have been a source of inspiration, motivation and second pair of eyes during the compiling of this work; Kevin L. A. Ewing, Cindy Washburn, Jerry, and Imani, just to name a few.

It is my sincere prayer that every person seeking truth finds it and that this book assists in setting them free from the spiritual bondage they may not have known has imprisoned them.

TABLE OF CONTENTS

Notes to Reader
Warning

Satan and his demons do not want you to read this book or obtain any knowledge of how they operate. Whether you believe this subject matter or not doesn't affect the real events that happened in the lives of many people. You may experience many distractions trying to get you not read the scriptures, say the prayers included and finished reading through to the end. To aid with this below is a prayer to arm you spiritually as you learn more about Spirit Spouses and the Kingdom of the Marine Spirits.

"Heavenly Father, I humbly ask that you shield and protect me as I read the material contained in this book. Give me Father, a clear mind to understand the contents and the spirit of discernment as I reflect on my life as revelation and knowledge are imparted into me. These things I ask and thank you for in the precious mighty name of your Son, Jesus Christ our Lord. Amen."

First, let us be clear, the spirit you IS THE REAL YOU. When our flesh body dies, our spirit will live on for eternity. Whatever takes place in the Spirit World manifests in the Physical World once a spirit and human makes a covenant/agreement. To stop these manifestations the covenant/agreement MUST be broken. This book is sectioned into two main parts.

The first addresses spirit spouses (marine spirits), how to identify if you are married to one, their attributes, and how the spiritual marriage occurred. The second part provides a deeper understanding of marine spirits. Their attributes, how to use the Word of God as a weapon against them, not only for yourself to remain free of these spirits but also to recognize and assist others in deliverance from them.

At the end are scriptures and a prayer to be set free from spiritual marriages.

KEY - Sex has powerful spiritual results. It joins together people that perform this act as **<u>one flesh</u>** through their souls, spirits, and bodies. It is why God said it was for marriage only and the Spirit World knows this, using man's ignorance to this for demonic possession and affliction through spirit spouses. The only other more powerful act is that of blood sacrifices/covenants.

Key Word Definitions:

Satan – who was called Lucifer in Heaven, name changed when he fell from grace. He orchestrates the activity of his spirit followers, who do his evil bidding upon mankind.

Repent – feel or express sincere regret or remorse about one's wrongdoing or sin.

Covenant - an agreement, contract, undertaking, commitment, guarantee, warrant, pledge, promise, bond.

Spouse - a husband or wife. Considered in relation to their partner, mate, consort, better half, other half.

Kingdom - a realm associated with or regarded as being under the control of a particular person or thing, domain, province, territory, arena, zone.

Marine - of, found in, or produced by the sea, seawater, saltwater, aquatic.

Spirit - the nonphysical part of a person regarded as a person's true self and is capable of surviving physical death or separation; a supernatural being.

CHAPTER ONE

What is a Spirit Spouse?

This type of spirit takes the form of a person, whose face specifically relates to you; often appearing with the face of someone familiar. The interactions of these spirit spouses are not limited to dreams alone. There are those that have had experiences with them physically appearing if only for brief periods. Many have detailed encounters with spirit spouses while sleeping, in what was so real that physical evidence remained upon waking.

They are very possessive, and their only intent is the utter destruction and death of all they marry through ungodly covenants. Their acts of adoration and love are only guises to keep their human victim from trying to sever the ties. Be not be deceived; they will do whatever to keep you from having a long lasting and meaningful relationship with another human being. Often, they will make single people take on a false repelling demeanor so that anyone interested in pursuing them will either slowly or suddenly lose interest.

Many people have experienced heartache after heartache from failed relationships. Understand that it is

God's will that you be in covenant with the one He has ordained so that together, you both bring Him glory. Read the contents of this book and in complete honesty with yourself and God, start the journey to deliverance and God's intended end for your life.

Per God, spirits are NOT to marry! Use these scriptures against them and to deepen your knowledge of God's Word; exercise your authority through Jesus Christ!

Matthew 22:29-32 New King James Version (NKJV)

29. Jesus answered and said to them, "You are mistaken, not knowing the Scriptures nor the power of God.

30. For in the resurrection they neither marry nor are given in marriage, but are like angels of God[a] in heaven.

31. But concerning the resurrection of the dead, have you not read what was spoken to you by God, saying,

32 'I am the God of Abraham, the God of Isaac, and the God of Jacob'?[b] God is not the God of the dead, but of the living."

Leviticus 19:19 New King James Version (NKJV)

19. 'You shall keep My statutes. You shall not let your livestock breed with another kind. You shall not sow your field with mixed seed. Nor shall a garment of mixed linen and wool come upon you.

Leviticus 19:19 clearly is demonstrating Gods command not to mix species. Human and spirits are not to physically join/produce.

CHAPTER TWO

The Attributes of a Spirit Spouse

- They are extremely stubborn, aggressive, and dangerous. Often when you begin to work on your deliverance from them, there can be physical injuries appearing on/in your body (scratched, bites, symptoms of illness with no medical confirmation, etc.).

- They are persistent, always working, so they don't offend Satan. They target all your weaknesses and use them against you.

- They are persuasive in having you do ungodly assignments, pushing people who have no discernment of sin.

- They are punctual and committed to their jobs, look at the consistency and time of your attacks; you will see their patterns are regular.

- They are liars and deceive. All gifts (physical gifts given by other people who have spirits active in their life and the Holy Spirit has warned you about the gift(s)/person), supernatural gifts (such as psychokinesis (moving things with your mind), telepathy, speaking to "the dead" etc., money, jobs etc. All they give is only for your complete destruction.

- They are productive, meaning they want to control all of your life in order to destroy you not just stopping at a percent of your life. They work to have 100 percent control.

- They are very powerful over their evil abilities and can greatly influence your dreams.

- They make you feel sexually excited even when no one is around. You follow through on the desire through masturbation; it is the spirit spouse wanting this to keep you bound. Also, this is one of the only ways for these spirits to enjoy pleasure, through a willing human flesh body.

- They will initiate you into being just like them – evil. Using such means as giving you strange dreams of being in unknown places, partaking in seemingly innocent practices. When you wake up, you are tired because spiritually they were using you.

- They will take away your glory and prosperity. Everything you own these spirits take, the spirit spouse does the opposite of God's law and subtracts.

1 Corinthians 11:3 New King James Version (NKJV)

3. But I want you to know that the head of every man is Christ, the head of woman is man, and the head of Christ is God.

- They can take away your spiritual power by weakening your prayer life. This will weaken you against their attacks taking you deeper into bondage/oppression by them.

- They can destroy, delay your physical marriage or block you from ever getting married. Any person that comes into your life will suddenly or eventually leave. They will make you hate the person you are to marry. Women having a desire to marry, they will kill that desire.

- They cause misfortune in your life. Everything works for others and not you, you are almost at the edge of a breakthrough but never actually get to the promise. They want you for themselves and don't want anyone else to have you.

John 10:10 King James Version (KJV)

10. The thief cometh not, but for to steal, and to kill, and to destroy: I am come that they might have life, and that they might have it more abundantly.

- They will see to it that you work hard, but no definite reward comes from your labor. As soon as you have anything, it is taken away by one means or another.

- They cause marital confusion....always confusion in your marriage if you do get to have a physical marriage.

- They are the enemy with killer motives; they kill your joy, peace, health, calling in life, virtue, marriages, etc.

- They violate the right of their victims as most are joined with them through unwilling means (blackmailed, manipulated); forced or done by another person's unknown act.

- They can entice with physical gifts. One way can be in the form of bribery.

- Mercy is far from them; they have none as their only goal is to destroy you.

- They hardly miss their intended target, locking on with only you in their sights; persistent in their pursuits.

- Often they appear with familiar faces, a tactic to lower the guard of their victims.

- They empower lust and decay in society. They offer worldly success, riches for which many people will compromise themselves for, continuously breeding immorality.

- Prostitutes are heavily used as strong bait to entangle their target. (Note a prostitute is anyone using their body for material gain. You don't have to be on a street corner; you can be someone that "appears respectable, normal, everyday person" however, you will do anything for material gain as well as career and/or social advancement).

CHAPTER THREE

How did These Spiritual Marriages Happen?

1. Someone in your family went to a witch or warlock and formed a covenant to have a child. A spirit opens the woman's womb and takes ownership of the child before birth, via spiritual marriage because of the covenant made with the spirit.

2. Sometimes family members go for protection over their family, and then the whole bloodline is now in the covenant, meaning all future generations will have spirit spouses.

3. Through inheritance from a parent that may not have even known they had a spirit spouse.

4. Can enter through rape or molestation of the victim and through heredity of spirits resulting from the rape or molestation that happened to an ancestor, abortion too.

    a. In this case, one would pray against any inherited curses as rape and molestation are widely used openings for spirit bonding. The result of the act has physiological effects even if the victim refuses to acknowledge them; they still manifest in areas of the victim's development.

b. Abortion is something that has been used by the "medical practitioner" as a means of aiding, whether knowingly or not, the continuation of human sacrifice. Blood represents life in the Physical World, and its power feeds the Spirit Realm. This is why often blood sacrifices were requested by God prior to Jesus shedding His on the cross. Aborted fetuses and placentas are used widely in the cosmetic/beauty (ingredients urea and collagen) industry as well as stolen by and sold to those practicing witchcraft.

5. Engaging in traditional dances using drums etc. at festivals/carnivals invoke spirits as dancers are dressed like fetish priests, wearing costumes, etc. This "marries" the family bloodline until someone takes a stand, repents for the ancestral sin, and comes against the altar erected. (Note: An altar does not necessarily have to be the traditional type – flat table-like surface, but can be anything used when the evil covenant was made. It can be a tree, a grave,

a certain spot outside or in a building, practically anything or anywhere). If you want to dance, do it for Jesus during your praise and worship time.

Either in your hometown or when you travel and come across such dancing, do not think that it is all for fun and/or entertainment. These dances invoke spirits who desire to possess a human body to have its way in the Physical World. The majority if not all of these dances, were passed down as a custom to give thanks and honor to one deity or another (other than God). So it is not only a medium for spirits to come upon or possess a person, but for a believer, they are "worshiping other gods."

A question was posed relating to belly dancing and similar forms of dancing......if you look at its history belly dancing was used as a means of enticement. The dance often puts viewers into a trance similar to how cobras affect their pray when "dancing" before they strike. Also, through history, it was the top form of dancing done throughout the world.

What about other types of performing you may wonder. Well, consider what type of "performance" it was....burlesque, for example, is also enticing, and if you looked at performers today, there is hardly any that are not dancing in order to keep their audience "captivated." Think of Herod's daughter (whose mother was Queen Herodias) who performed for him and his royal guests, enticing all that watched. She asked for the head of John the Baptist per her mother's instructions, as Herod said anything she wanted he would give if she'd dance for him.

Mathew 14:6 New King James Version (NKJV)

6. But when Herod's birthday was celebrated, the daughter of Herodias danced before them and pleased Herod.

6. Sexual perversion; pornography, masturbation opens the door for a spirit spouse. Sleeping around, having sexual intercourse, performing sexual acts when you are not married (and to your physical spouse) – opens the door for them to enter your life and pollute your spirit. **Everyone you have sex with <u>outside of marriage</u> you open yourself up to the spirits of the last seven people each of them has had sex with - DO THE MATH.**

7. Through tattooing and piercing. For women, **one set** of ear piercing is common for adornment.

However, through history, men wore piercings in their ears as a sign of being owned, slave, and as a sign of homosexuality. Also, the question people should ask themselves is why you have so many earrings in your ears, is it to "follow a fashion trend?" There is great danger in "following trends" as few are new under the sun and have roots in very old customs.....people hardly study for themselves, just "follow along."

Piercing, in particular, are those that are in other places about the body besides the earlobes. Some people have them to increase pleasure; others again follow trends. Cutting and piercings are old customs done by many other deity worshipers, primarily for the dead.

Leviticus 19:28 New King James Version (NKJV)

28. Ye shall not make any cuttings in your flesh for the dead, nor print any marks upon you (*tattoo*): I am the LORD.

8. Indecent dressing - modest dressing is key (not constantly old-fashioned, wearing skirts to the ankles and turtleneck type blouses!) Overly sexy

clothing that shows a lot of your bodies shape, leaving little or nothing to the imagination. This form of dressing not only attracts a man or woman to like you but can also attract spirits the same way. You may need to do a cleaning out of your closet. Pray and let God direct you through the Holy Spirit what to do concerning your wardrobe.

9. Also, there are some hairstyles that are also appealing to spirits, the cutting of shapes and designs in the hair (similar to tattooing), women taking on man-looking hairstyles and men fixing their hair in feminine ways.....

Hair extensions to conform to the world's standards of "beautiful":

   a. In India, one of the top countries supplying hair for extensions, they believe that the "bad energy from past lives is in the hair" which stems from the belief of the following:

> "So that he could pay for his wedding to the goddess Parvati, Vishnu made a deal with the Treasurer of the gods, Kubera who demanded a very high-interest rate. Kubera decided over several thousands of years the debt would

be paid. Generations throughout
the centuries have continued to
pay off the debt with money,
jewelry and often the only thing
of value left, their hair. "

The hair shaved from the heads of the
thousands that flock the Hindu Temples is
dedicated to its gods; also known as tonsure
(ton-suree). The hair eventually ends up in
possession of companies worldwide that
retail it as hair extensions, once purchased
from "middle-men."

On average in a month these "middle-men"
receive about 5 tons of hair at about $200 to
$300 USD, which is what they pay per kilo
(about 2 pounds) from the temple managers,
who oversee the gathering of hair shavings.
Retail extensions are generally sold in
ounces, so the cost of the "middle-men" that
sell companies who then mark up the price
and retail it to customers, is about $8.33 to
$12.50 per ounce. The demand continues to
increase year over year in this billion dollar
industry. How much are you paying per

ounce and I don't mean just financially but spiritually as well?

10. Jewelry that is made in the shape of symbols used for other god worship and others you may not know of, have been offered unto other gods! PRAY over the things you buy and if not sure ask God if it is acceptable to Him. He will give you peace or disturb your spirit in response.

Understand many stores and business owners ARE NOT serving the same God as you, The Most High. They have dedicated their business to other gods and all that they sell. This also goes for the food you purchase – remember to ALWAYS bless and sanctify your food in the name of Jesus! If you cover yourself with the Blood of Jesus daily, you will be protected from the unknown covenants that try to establish themselves with you through just everyday life activities.

Too many spend a lot of time concerned making their outward appearance more attractive than how they look on the inside. Often they are late to appointments because they have to be

"perfect" before everyone sees them. See 1 Peter 3 below:

1 Peter 3: 1- 7 New King James Version (NKJV)

Submission to Husbands (for wives and single women not yet married)

1. Wives, likewise, be submissive to your own husbands, that even if some do not obey the word, they, without a word, may be won by the conduct of their wives,

2. When they observe your chaste conduct accompanied by fear.

3. Do not let your adornment be merely outward— arranging the hair, wearing gold, or putting on fine apparel

4. Rather let it be the hidden person of the heart, with the incorruptible beauty of a gentle and quiet spirit, which is very precious in the sight of God.

5. For in this manner, in former times, the holy women who trusted in God also adorned themselves, being submissive to their own husbands,

6. As Sarah obeyed Abraham, calling him lord, whose daughters you are if you do good and are not afraid with any terror.

Some Dream Indicators of Spirit Spouses Active in Your Life

- You are missing your menstrual period in a dream

- Having a prolonged pregnancy (beyond nine months)

- Disappearance of wedding ring

- The loss of a job or valuables not long after getting married

- When your loving physical spouse has suddenly become your enemy

- Being pregnant in a dream

- Breastfeeding in a dream and seeing your breasts secreting milk

- Inability to conceive

- Having bad body odor in a dream

- Constant wet dreams

- Getting married in a dream

- Inability to maintain a holy life in a dream; going back to doing what you did before accepting Jesus Christ as Lord and Savior

- Always being dumped by a partner of a serious relationship; one you had plans to either become engaged to or marry in the future

- Feeling tired every morning upon waking; due to the physical demands the spirit spouse put you through when you should have been experiencing a peaceful and restful sleep

CHAPTER FOUR

The Significance of Water

Being "saved" – accepting Jesus Christ, believing He died for your sins is not enough, **you must be born again** (having the "renewed mind of Jesus Christ).

John 3:1-21 New King James Version (NKJV)

The New Birth

1. There was a man of the Pharisees named Nicodemus, a ruler of the Jews.

2. This man came to Jesus by night and said to Him, "Rabbi, we know that You are a teacher come from God; for no one can do these signs that You do unless God is with him."

3. Jesus answered and said to him, "Most assuredly, I say to you, unless one is born again, he cannot see the kingdom of God."

4. Nicodemus said to Him, "How can a man be born when he is old? Can he enter a second time into his mother's womb and be born?"

5. Jesus answered, "Most assuredly, I say to you, unless one is born of water and the Spirit, he cannot enter the kingdom of God.

6. That which is born of the flesh is flesh, and that which is born of the Spirit is spirit.

7. Do not marvel that I said to you, 'You must be born again.'

8. The wind blows where it wishes, and you hear the sound of it, but cannot tell where it comes from and where it goes. So is everyone who is born of the Spirit."

9. Nicodemus answered and said to Him, "How can these things be?"

10. Jesus answered and said to him, "Are you the teacher of Israel, and do not know these things?

11. Most assuredly, I say to you, We speak what We know and testify what We have seen, and you do not receive Our witness.

12. If I have told you earthly things and you do not believe, how will you believe if I tell you heavenly things?

13. No one has ascended to heaven but He who came down from heaven, that is, the Son of Man who is in heaven.[a]

14. And as Moses lifted up the serpent in the wilderness, even so must the Son of Man be lifted up,

15. that whoever believes in Him should not perish but[b] have eternal life.

16. For God so loved the world that He gave His only begotten Son, that whoever believes in Him should not perish but have everlasting life.

17. For God did not send His Son into the world to condemn the world, but that the world through Him might be saved.

18. "He who believes in Him is not condemned; but he who does not believe is condemned already, because he has not believed in the name of the only begotten Son of God.

19. And this is the condemnation, that the light has come into the world, and men loved darkness rather than light, because their deeds were evil.

20. For everyone practicing evil hates the light and does not come to the light, lest his deeds should be exposed.

21. But he who does the truth comes to the light, that his deeds may be clearly seen, that they have been done in God."

Isaiah 5:13 New King James Version (NKJV)

13. Therefore my people are gone into captivity, because they have no knowledge; their honorable men are famished, and their multitude dried up with thirst.

Psalm 29:3 and 10 New King James Version (NKJV)

3. The voice of the Lord *is* over the waters; The God of glory thunders; The Lord *is* over many   waters.

10. The Lord sat *enthroned* at the Flood, And the Lord sits as King forever.

The above scriptures show how a person's way of thinking is vital to understanding things of the Spirit World. Without the renewed/changed mind of Jesus

Christ in us, we have no chance to comprehend what is happening all around us and to us from beyond what we can be aware of using our physical senses. If you have not accepted Jesus Christ as your Lord and Savior up to this period in your life, the information in this book and available from other sources will not resonate with your spirit (your true self). Until you have done so, the full revelation **will not be yours**.

You are encouraged, however, to continue reading, and it is my sincere prayer that your spiritual eyes will be opened, and you will accept Jesus Christ as your Lord and Savior. Understand though that salvation is a gift and not something given based on anything you have done.

Ephesians 2:8-9 New King James Version (NKJV)

8. For by grace you have been saved through faith, and that not of yourselves; *it is* the gift of God,

9. not of works, lest anyone should boast.

To receive the gift of salvation, repeat the following with a sincere heart:

"Jesus is Lord, and I believe that God raised him from him from dead."

Bible reference for salvation prayer:

Romans 10:9-10 New King James Version (NKJV)

9. that if you confess with your mouth the Lord Jesus and believe in your heart that God has raised Him from the dead, you will be saved.

10. For with the heart one believes unto righteousness, and with the mouth confession is made unto salvation.

Water is Key; Water is Life

* Both doctors and scientists have confirmed that up to 60% of the human body's weight consists of water.

* 72% of the earth's surface is made up of water

* Man needs water for everything. He can survive without food for up to three weeks. However, he cannot go that long without drinking water.

* Man uses water for drinking, bathing, cleaning, cooking, farming and medical treatment.

* Water exists in the form of rain, streams, lakes, rivers, and oceans.

* The Bible also states that the foundation of the whole earth is upon the waters, (Psalms 24:2).

Psalm 24:2 New King James Version (NKJV)

2. For He has founded it upon the seas, And established it upon the waters.

So if water is so vital and significant in the lives of mankind, it is no wonder that Satan uses it as a means to gain his worship and send his attacks from. His intent from just before his fall from Heaven (known as Lucifer then) was to lift his throne above that of The Most High. After his fall, knowing what his fate in the end will be, he set out to destroy that which God holds precious; us!

Isaiah 14:12-13 New King James Version (NKJV)

The Fall of Lucifer

12. "How you are fallen from heaven, O Lucifer,[a] son of the morning!
How you are cut down to the ground, You who weakened the nations!
13. For you have said in your heart: 'I will ascend into heaven, I will exalt my throne above the stars of God; I will also sit on the mount of the congregation On the farthest sides of the north;

Revelation 20:10 New King James Version (NKJV)
The Fate of Satan, the Devil (Lucifer)

10. The devil, who deceived them, was cast into the lake of fire and brimstone where[a] the beast and the false prophet are. And they will be tormented day and night forever and ever.

CHAPTER FIVE

What is a Marine Spirit?

Whatever you get is from Satan, not from God when you commit/covenant with one i.e. Your gifts (physical and spiritual), jobs, apparent success. All are designed to give you a destructive end.

Lilith seeks to find rest in a physical body. Physical evidence of the presence of a marine spirit is the placement of the snake in their body. As deliverance prayers are spoken, the one who is praying for self-deliverance or being prayed over for deliverance, more often than not will experience pain from the snakes squeezing on the part of the body it is coiled around. Such as the leg, waist, arm, back, neck. Many have also experienced such pain while seeking Godly knowledge and wisdom that would eventually lead them to having to choose between staying spiritually bound or being set free.

The pain is because the snake spirit doesn't want to leave the body and uses the pain as a distraction from focusing on God's Word. It is important for you to understand that the snake has always been subtle, a trait used throughout history and still today when things opposite to the will of God manifest in the Physical World.

Genesis 3:1 New King James Version (NKJV)
The Temptation and Fall of Man

3. Now the serpent was more cunning than any beast of the field which the LORD God had made.

Yoga (all forms) has exploded on the world as a form of exercise, relaxation; alternative means to help you focus. This subtle, deceptive practice has made millions slaves to the snake spirit. Sadly, many Christians and Churches have allowed yoga into their midst and undoubtedly, have not studied the full history of this practice.

God's Word says we are to think on good things NOT empty our minds which allows for ALL types of spiritual take overs. In essence, the power of yoga comes from the **Kundalini** *(Sanskrit for "coiled serpent")*, an enormous reserve of untapped potential within each of us, activated around the sacrum or "sacred bone" at the base of the spine.

Philippians 4:8 King James Version (KJV)

8. Finally, brethren, whatsoever things are true, whatsoever things are honest, whatsoever things are just, whatsoever things are pure, whatsoever things are lovely, whatsoever things are of good report; if there be any virtue, and if there be any praise, think on these things.

Kundalini Yoga is an ancient **technology** sometimes referred to as the mother of all yoga's and arguably the most powerful yoga there is. As brought to the West in 1969 by *Yogi Bhajan*, it produces results up to 16 times faster than Hatha Yoga. My next book will cover this topic in fuller detail, explaining its root origins and the way it goes completely against the Word of God, The Most High.

"Technology can be viewed as an activity that forms or changes culture."
(1a)

Isaiah 34:14 - 17 New King James Version (NKJV)

14. The wild beasts of the desert shall also meet with the jackals, And the wild goat shall bleat to its companion; Also the **night creature** shall rest there, **And find for herself a place of rest.**

15. There the arrow snake shall make her nest and lay *eggs,* And hatch, and gather *them* under her shadow; There also shall the hawks be gathered, Everyone with her mate.

16. "Search from the book of the Lord, and read: Not one of these shall fail; Not one shall lack her mate. For My mouth has commanded it, and His Spirit has gathered them.

17. He has cast the lot for them, And His hand has divided it among them with a measuring line. They shall possess it forever; From generation to generation they shall dwell in it."

The above scripture, Isaiah 34:14-17, is the prophecy that Isaiah spoke to all nations regarding the judgment against those that opposed God. Note how the word **"shall"** is repeated, meaning that what is spoke **will happen**.

So in essence, Lilith's eggs (offspring) will all find a mate (spouse). This would help to explain the spiritual infestation (demonic pregnancies) on the earth regardless of where you live as this judgment again was to all opposing nations. This can be seen clearly (if one were just to pay attention), in several countries and businesses around the world.

Mami Wata (Mother Water)

Mami Wata (Mother Water) is celebrated throughout much of Africa and the African Atlantic area. Mami Wata's powerful and pervasive presence results from a number of factors. It was and still is believed that she can bring good fortune in the form of money, and as a "capitalist", her power was increased between the fifteenth and twentieth centuries, during the era of Africa's growing trade with the rest of the world.

It was through the countless millions of enslaved Africans who were torn from their homeland and forcibly carried across the Atlantic between the sixteenth and nineteenth centuries as part of this "trade" brought with them their beliefs, practices, and arts honoring Mami Wata and other ancestral deities.

Reestablished, revisualized, and revitalized by the countless people displaced from their homeland, Mami Wata emerged in new communities and under different guises, among them:

- Lasirèn (in Haiti)

- Yemanja (in Brazil)

- Santa Marta la Dominadora (the Dominican Republic)

- Sanse (Puerto Rico)

- Oxum (Latin America) also known as Oshun (who Beyonce dressed up as during the pregnancy with her twins and many pregnant women have started to do the same).

African-based faiths continue to flourish in communities throughout the world, many being introduced through "entertainment" for easier "infiltration" of a knowledge-less, non-studying world.

Mami Wata's powers, extend far beyond economic gain. She is served by followers to assist in the area of procreation—infertility, impotence, or infant mortality. Some are drawn to her as an irresistible seductive presence who offers the pleasures and powers that accompany devotion to a spiritual force.

Still, she represents danger, for a relationship/covenant with Mami Wata often requires a substantial sacrifice, such as the life of a family member or celibacy in the physical realm (as any and all sex will be through spirit spouses). If celibacy is not part of the covenant, it is believed Mami Wata can assist both men and women; arrange for their sexual desires and preferences to become a reality (again sex being used to form a strong covenant). Mami Wata is also known to provide both a spiritual and professional avenue for women to become powerful priestesses and healers of both psycho-spiritual and physical ailments. She can also assert females status in generally male-dominated societies.

This can be seen in places where women are hardly taught to respect their husbands, even as single women on the dating scene. They are instead often feed the mindset of being equal in authority to men and in some instances, not even needing a man as long as they "get theirs". This goes against the order for which God created men and women.

Genesis 2:18, 22 – 24 King James Version (KJV)

18. And the Lord God said, It is not good that the man should be alone; I will make him an help meet for him.

21. And the Lord God caused a deep sleep to fall upon Adam, and he slept: and he took one of his ribs, and closed up the flesh instead thereof;

22. And the rib, which the Lord God had taken from man, made he a woman, and brought her unto the man.

23. And Adam said, This is now bone of my bones, and flesh of my flesh: she shall be called Woman, because she was taken out of Man.

24. Therefore shall a man leave his father and his mother, and shall cleave unto his wife: and they shall be one flesh.

Sadly, as these women age, they find out just how emotionally destructive this mindset has become in their lives. Women are the emotional balance to the relationship. Without Gods appointed man in her life, she will eventually work herself to death or practice whatever she can find to do in an attempt to fill the void and temporarily stop from being overwhelmed by her emotions. Men are the rational balance to women. The flip side to this is also evident in many of society's men. They seek to attain success in all areas except that of family, trying to fill the emotional void that only Gods appointed woman can fill in their life.

The constant socioeconomic changes, and the pressures of trying to survive in many parts of the world, have increased the need for the curative powers of Mami Wata priestesses and priests. Even without the general understanding of what is going on, who these "undercover" priestesses and priests are, masses of people are obeying their subtle directions. Examine the things you see on television, social media websites, hear in the music being played in public places, on the radio, in the cars passing you by on the streets.

A better understanding of the subtleness would be how worshippers of Mami Wata have selected local as well as global images, arts, ideas, and actions, interpreted them according to indigenous precepts, presented them with new meanings, and then **"re-presented them"** in different and compelling ways to serve their own specific aesthetic, devotional, social, economic, and political aspirations.

Mami Wata is often portrayed with the head and torso of a woman and the tail of a fish (Dona Fish). Half-fish and half-human, Mami Wata overlaps earth and water; culture and nature.

She may also take the form of a snake charmer, sometimes in combination with her mermaid attributes and sometimes separate from them. As difficult as it may be for some to grasp the concept of this challenging water spirit in her "singular" manifestation, the existence of Mami Watas and Papi Watas (mermen) must also be acknowledged.

These spirits are included in a vast and uncountable "school" of indigenous African water spirits (both female and male); each with specific local names and individual personalities. These other spirits are honored in intricate systems of beliefs and practices which may or may not be the same as attributed to the water spirit, Mami Wata.

Mythical Origin of Mami Wata

The mystical pantheon of Mami Wata deities are often pictured in their most ancient primordial aspects as a mermaid, half-human or either half-fish or half-reptile. Mermaids are not recent phenomena in African history. For example, according to the Dogon Tribes' creation myth, they attribute the creation of the world to

mermaid/mermen like creatures whom they call Nommos. They claimed to have known about the existence of these mermaid-like divinities for more than 4,000 years.

Nommos means "to make one drink." They are usually depicted as amphibious, hermaphroditic, fish-like creatures. Folk art depictions of the Nommos show creatures with humanoid upper torsos, legs/feet, and a fish-like lower torso and tail. The Nommos are also referred to as "Masters of the Water", "the Monitors", and "the Teachers".

Also according to Dogon mythology, the ancient home of these (originally crude) reptilian (half-woman/half-men/fish) pantheon of water spirits is believed to be the obscure and celebrated star system in the belt of Orion known as Sirius (or Sopdet, Sothis), more popularly known as the "Dog Star" of Isis. When asked where their ancestors obtained these stories of mermaids and mermen, they quickly point to ancient Egypt (Griaule, 1997, Winters 1985, p. 50-64, Temple 1999, p.303-304). Mermaid/mermen "nymphs" worshiped as goddesses and gods born from the sea are numerous in ancient African cultures history and spiritual mythology.

So then, why do those who have pledged to fraternities and sororities say they only serve God, The Most High when they have taken oaths to these (and other) "Greek Gods" as part of their inanition? If the actions and pledges made have not be renounced, the evil spirits you came into covenant with still have a legal right to your life, regardless if you claim to be a Christian or not. The covenants MUST be broken in order to be free.

Most Nommos were honored and respected for being "bringers of divine law" and for establishing the theological, moral, social, political, economic and, cultural foundation, to regulating the overflow of the Nile, and regulating the ecology i.e., establishing days for success at sailing and fishing, hunting, planting etc., and for punishment by sending devastating floods when laws and taboos were violated.

However, just as not all serpents were revered, not all mermaids/mermen were considered "good." In one story, the famed London, Naturalists Henry Lee (1883) recounts that "in the sea of Angola mermaids are frequently caught which resemble the human species. They are taken in nets, and killed . . . and are heard to shriek and cry like women (p. 22)."

Ancient Origins of Name "Mami Wata"

The name "Mami Wata," was believed by Western scholars to be a derivative either directly from pidgin English, or is an anglicize version of the two words "mommy/mammy" and "water." However, though phonetically similar to the English words, the name "Mami Wata" does not have its linguistic roots or any cultural, mythological or historical origins in the West. Mami Wata are ancient African deities whose root origins and name can be traced linguistically through the languages of Africa.

According to some renowned scholars, the name "Mami Wata" was originally formulated in ancient Egypt and Mesopotamia, and is derived from a composite of two African words, "Mami," and "Wata." Both words are rooted in the ancient Egyptian and Ethiopian (Coptic), Galla and Demotic languages. "Mami" is derived from "Ma" or "Mama," meaning "truth/wisdom," and "Wata" is a corruption of not an English, but the ancient Egyptian word "Uati," (or "Uat-ur" meaning ocean water), and the Khosian ("Hottentot") "Ouata" meaning "water."

Further, we discover from Mesopotamian myths that the first great water goddess in the story of the Creation Flood was known as "Mami," (Mami Aruru) as she was known in ancient Babylonian prayers as being the creator of human life (Dalley 2000, p. 51-16, Stone 1976, p. 7,219). Interestingly, the Sumerian city-state of Ur was a part of Mesopotamia, an area where a huge number of gods and goddesses were worshiped. This was where Abram (Abraham) was from and where God told him to move from and go to a place He would show Abram.

An ancient female water spirit sometimes referred to as Tingoi/Njaloi epitomizes ideal yet unattainable beauty, power, and goodness. She presides over female initiation rites among various peoples in Sierra Leone and Liberia, including Mende, Temne, Bullom, Vai, Gola, Dei, Krim, Kissi, and Bassa (Lamp 1985, Boone 1986, Phillips 1995:37). Tingoi/Njaloi is often likened to a mermaid (Phillips 1995:53–4), and Muslim Mende peoples speak of her as a female jina, or spirit, with the lower body of a fish. Sowei/Nowo initiation headdresses from this region offer deep and complex allusions to Tingoi/Njaloi as well as to social practices and cosmic forces.

These headdresses are worn by women elders during the initiations of young girls. A zigzag motif found on the forehead of some of these headdresses may be a glyph for water, and young Sande/Bondo girls are said to "go under the water" during the first part of their initiation (Boone 1986:50, 170). Among the Temne, as Frederick Lamp notes, "water is the gestating fluid of rebirth, called, in the esoteric language of initiation, yankoila, 'Mother Water'" (1985:42).

HONORING THE SEA
Santa Monica Beach, 10/1/11

Photo : Offering to Yemanja, the Afro-Brazilian deity of the Sea, **at Santa Monica Beach, (California, USA)** led by Swing Brazil Tribe and elders from Bahia, Brazil.

Part of Honoring the Sea, the opening ceremony to the 2011 World Festival of Sacred Music **in Los Angeles.**

In Brazil, offerings to Yemanja take place each year on February 2 in Salvador, Bahia. In Rio de Janeiro, offerings to Yemanja are a highly celebrated New Year ritual.

On YouTube:
https://www.youtube.com/watch?time_continue=12&v=Q_hxBAHf7Qc

PRIMARY FUNCTION

On a basic level, in the family, Mami Wata's primary role in the life of the devotee/initiate is "healing," by helping the initiate to achieve wholeness both spiritually and materially in their lives. Mami Wata is also responsible for protection, emotional, and mental healing, spiritual growth/balance, and maintaining social order by assuring that sacred laws imposed on both the initiate and the family in which she/he lives is maintained → covenant!

When these requirements are met, Mami Wata often blesses the initiate (and family) with material wealth. "Wealth" being relative to assuring that the family has the basic needs of survival, such as shelter, food, clothing, medicine and funds to maintain them. Or, wealth could mean achieving great riches through some profession or spiritual gifts the initiate might possess.

Far from being the over-embellished, "seductress" or "god/dess of love" so over-emphasized by western anthropologists, Mami Wata is primarily known to produce Africa's great seers, prophetesses, prophets, scribes, herbalists, healers, orators, mystics, etc. They are also known as the protector of mothers and children, and of abused women, and the "bringer of fertility" to both men and to barren women. They are even known in ancient history as being the "protector of sacred prostitutes", meaning those African priestesses whose role was to join the "uncivilized invader/foreign groups" by "spreading the ache" (have sexual desire for) of the African god and goddesses.

So as the people of Africa spread out into the world through slave trade, so did the curses of these worshiped god and goddesses.

Mermaid which is found in Beaufort, SC that was part of a 2006 art project, "Beaufort's Big Swim". It is entitled Mami Wata.

Mami Wata Icons in the Twentieth Century

Between the fifteenth and nineteenth centuries, the vast majority of visitors from overseas that Africans encountered were European or American. By the early twentieth century, however, as Europeans established a colonial presence in Africa, other peoples from European-influenced areas, such as Lebanon and the British colony of India, began to arrive. They came as traders and, like the Europeans before them, were associated by Africans with wealth from overseas.

In the 1930s and 1940s (possibly inspired in part by Mahatma Gandhi's successful campaign for India's independence and by African soldiers serving in South Asia during World War II), Indian material culture in the form of images in books, pamphlets, films, and popular devotional chromolithographs (Bae 2003), as well as the ritual practices of Indian traders in Africa, came to have a profound impact on Mami Wata worshipers, their icons, and their ritual actions.

A new episode in the development of the visual culture of Mami Wata began in the 1940s–1950s. The popularity of the snake charmer lithograph and the presence of Indian merchants (and films) in West Africa had led to a growing fascination with Indian prints of Hindu gods and goddesses. In various places, especially along the Ghana-Nigeria coast, people began to interpret these deities as representations of a host of Mami Wata spirits associated with specific bodies and levels of water.

Joseph Kossivi Ahiator (b. 1956, Aflao, Ghana)."Indian King of Mami
Wata," 2005 Pigment, cloth; 267cm (105") Fowler Museum
X2005.5.1; Museum Purchase Ghanaian artist Joseph Kossivi
Ahiator, inspired by a Hindu print of Vishnu, created this complex
painting of a host of Mami Wata spirits that he calls "India Spirits."

Kossivi was born with India spirits and he visits India
often, sometimes in his dreams, sometimes while at the beach along
Ghana's coast. In 2005 Kossivi had vivid dreams of a nineteen-headed
Indian king spirit together with his nine-headed queen. He dreamed
that he was swimming with them in the ocean and thereafter called the
male "King of Mami Wata" and his queen "NaKrishna."

He has gathered these spirits under the ancient African celestial
rainbow serpent deity Dan Aida Wedo, thus forging links between
Africa, India, the sea, and ultimately the African Atlantic where
Dambala Wedo continues to be venerated by Haitians and others.

Some countries/businesses that bear the mark of these spirits. This is why it is important to pray daily before engaging in your daily activities.

"Chicken of the Sea"
Formerly USA owned, now owned by a Thailand Group

"Mami Wata"
Washington, DC swimwear company

"Siren Diving" United Kingdom diving company

"Starbucks"
Seattle, Washington coffee company

Remember to always ask God in Jesus name to sanctify/bless your food and drinks. Also, that of all merchandise you purchase either for yourself or as a gift to others.

CHAPTER SIX

How do Marine Spirits Enter a Person?

Psalm 27:10 New King James Version (NKJV)

10. When my father and my mother forsake me, Then the Lord will take care of me.

A common way is by rejection, which is **opposite** to God's Word. Thus a person develops the following:

- Fear of rejection, self-rejection, fear of judgement, nervousness
- Self-accusation, compulsive confessions, self-pity
- Jealousy and envy
- Lust, fantasy lust, harlotry, perverseness
- Insecurity, inferiority complex
- False compassion, false responsibility
- Depression, despair, discouragement, hopelessness
- Suicidal thoughts (suicide)
- Guilt, unworthiness and shame
- Pride, perfection (perfectionist)
- Unfairness

- Withdrawal, pouting, timid, shyness, loneness, sensitivity

- Unreality, fantasy day dreams, vivid imaginations

- Self-awareness

If any listed applies to you, be sure to call them out whenever you decide to perform either self-deliverance or have a strong believer in Jesus Christ pray for your deliverance over you.

CHAPTER SEVEN

The Attributes of a Marine Spirit

1 Corinthians 6:15-16 New King James Version (NKJV)

15. Do you not know that your bodies are members of Christ? Shall I then take the members of Christ and make them members of a harlot? Certainly not!

16. Or do you not know that he who is joined to a harlot is one body with her? For "the two," He says, "shall become one flesh

17. But he who is joined to the Lord is one spirit with Him.

By understanding who you are spiritually joined with, you have the first important weapon in either making the change or strengthening your spirit man.

Some signs that a marine spirit is at work are:

- Breaking up marriages
- Spouses hating each other (or just one showing signs of hate for their spouse)
- Miscarriages

- Impotence (low sperm count)

- Hardship (just can't get ahead in life no matter how hard you work)

- Financial failures (you make money but cannot keep it long)

- Marriage distress (constant fussing and fighting, can't seem to agree)

- Sex in dreams (if it's your spouse IT IS NOT THEM but a familiar spirit disguised as them)

- Wrong decisions (they keep you from attaining the wisdom of God)

- Neglect (they will cause you not to want to study God's Word)

- Swimming or seeing waters and rivers in your dreams

- Missing menstrual cycles in your dreams

- In the natural you have shortened or prolonged menstrual cycles

- Breast feeding in your dreams

- Having a family in dreams

- You are shopping with men or women in a dream

- Dreams relating to marriage

- Being pregnant in your dream

- You have a baby in a dream

- Seeing a man sleeping by your side

- You are left at the alter or in public places

With regard to "neglecting" the studying of God's Word, the marine spirit doesn't want you to know this is a vital weapon against them....

Job 7:12 New King James Version (NKJV)

12. *Am* I a sea, or a sea serpent, That You set a guard over me?

Satan loves to tag team with the spirits of fear and sexual immorality. The experience in dreams often referred to as "night terrors, sleep terrors, sleep paralysis, night visitor or being hagged"; feeling awake but unable to move.

There are people who experience the awareness that something or someone is near or next to them while awake.

Then there are those that have experiences feeling something moving in their bed and strange voices and sounds when they are on the verge of REM sleep or in it.

However, the promises of God will be fulfilled as it relates to all evil:

Zechariah 9:3-5 New King James Version (NKJV)

3. For Tyre built herself a tower, Heaped up silver like the dust, And gold like the mire of the streets.

4. **Behold, the Lord will cast her out; He will destroy her power in the sea, And she will be devoured by fire.**

5. Ashkelon shall see *it* and fear; Gaza also shall be very sorrowful; And Ekron, for He dried up her expectation. The king shall perish from Gaza, And Ashkelon shall not be inhabited.

Tyrus (a water spirit) Ashkelon (a city in Israel) - so those that are embracing evil spirits shall also be destroyed

PRAYER is MUCH MORE

than just a quick sentence or two in the morning, night, at meals, when we need a breakthrough or miracle! It is a **LIFESTYLE** of CONSTANT FELLOWSHIP with the **FATHER** through His **SON, JESUS** by the **HOLY SPIRIT.**

So if you love your spouse like yourself – you won't be open to spirit spouses gaining easy access to you. **NOTE:** the husband is the one that represents physical authority in the family.

Ephesians 5:25, 28 New King James Version (NKJV)

25. Husbands, love your wives, just as Christ also loved the church and gave Himself for her,

28. So husbands ought to love their own wives as their own bodies; he who loves his wife loves himself.

Ephesians 5:32-33 New King James Version (NKJV)

32. This is a great mystery, but I speak concerning Christ and the church.

33. Nevertheless let each one of you in particular so love his own wife as himself, and let the wife *see* that she respects *her* husband.

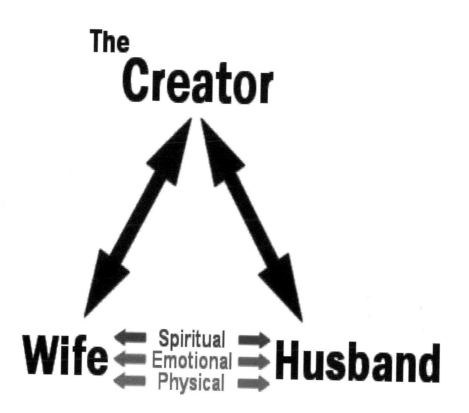

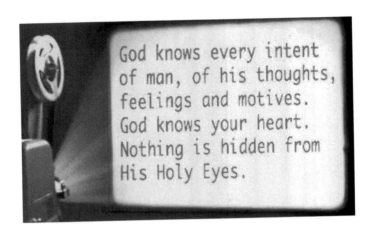

Psalm 139:1-7 New Century Version (NCV)

God Knows Everything

1. Lord, you have examined me and know all about me.

2 . You know when I sit down and when I get up. You know my thoughts before I think them.

3. You know where I go and where I lie down. You know everything I do.

4. Lord, even before I say a word, you already know it.

5. You are all around me—in front and in back - and have put your hand on me.

6. Your knowledge is amazing to me; it is more than I can understand.

7. Where can I go to get away from your Spirit? Where can I run from you?

CHAPTER EIGHT

Demonic Dream Assistance

This is when you're physically tired and decide to put off rebuking demonic attacks. For example it is very early in the morning, say at 3am and you are awaken, deciding to deal with covenants made in your dream when you wake up some time later. Understand that though you are sleeping for several hours a day, the Spirit World never sleeps.

Do not fall for this trick. Delaying the breaking of covenants is extremely dangerous because the spirits are counting on you to not act immediately (demonstrating agreement) so they can make their plans manifest in the physical. Remember not everything is about you; there are others whose destinies are on the line.

The human subconscious is quite extraordinary. Many tire themselves for one reason or another and gladly accept whatever quality of sleep they get. This is dangerous! Spirits know and understand this and wait until humans fall into REM sleep. Once you are there, they start their attacks as it is the deepest sleep and the human subconscious is wide open for manipulation. The flip side is God also communicates and covenants with humans while sleeping. However, it is not necessary for The Most

High to wait for humans to reach REM sleep in order to give revelation!

Definition of REM Sleep - Rapid eye movement **sleep** (**REM sleep**, REMS) is a unique phase of sleep in mammals and birds, characterized by random/rapid movement of the eyes, accompanied with low muscle tone throughout the body, and the propensity of the sleeper to dream vividly.

So to reiterate the above stated importance of rebuking, coming against any evil covenants made in your dreams:

- **REPENT** because there is a LEGAL right for the spirit to be there

- **REBUKE** immediately any demonic activity that just happened in your dream(s)! Come against the covenant just made even if you cannot remember it.

- **CAST THE SPIRIT OUT** in the name of Jesus, plead the blood of Jesus over you and pray on the whole Armor of God so you can return to sleep. *NOTE: you should always pray on the whole Armor of God before sleeping (this includes naps).*

- **NEXT** come into agreement with God for any covenants in our dreams (even if you don't remember them) so that His perfect will can activate in your life.

Matthew 26:41 New King James Version (NKJV)

41. Watch and pray, lest you enter into temptation. The spirit indeed *is* willing, but the flesh *is* weak."

1 Corinthians 3:16-17 New King James Version (NKJV)

16. Do you not know that you are the temple of God and that the Spirit of God dwells in you? 17 If anyone defiles the temple of God, God will destroy him. For the temple of God is holy, which temple you are.

Ephesians 6:10-18 New International Version (NIV)

The Armor of God

10. Finally, be strong in the Lord and in his mighty power.

11. Put on the full armor of God, so that you can take your stand against the devil's schemes. 12. For our struggle is not against flesh and blood, but against the rulers, against the authorities, against the powers of this dark world and against the spiritual forces of evil in the heavenly realms.

13. Therefore put on the full armor of God, so that when the day of evil comes, you may be able to stand your ground, and after you have done everything, to stand.

14. Stand firm then, with **the belt of truth** buckled around your waist, with **the breastplate of righteousness** in place,

15. and with your **feet** fitted **(covered) with** the readiness that comes from **the gospel of peace**.

16. In addition to all this, take up **the shield of faith**, with which you can extinguish all the flaming arrows of the evil one.

17. Take **the helmet of salvation and the sword of the Spirit**, which is the word of God.

18. And pray in the Spirit on all occasions with all kinds of prayers and requests. With this in mind, be alert and always keep on praying for all the Lord's people.

Armour of God

Wherefore take unto you the whole armour of God, that ye may be able to withstand in the evil day, and having done all, to stand (Ephesians 6:13 KJV).

Helmet of Salvation
(Ephesians 6:17)

Breastplate of Righteousness
(Ephesians 6:14)

Belt of Truth
(Ephesians 6:14)

Shield of Faith
(Ephesians 6:16)

Sword of the Spirit
(Ephesians 6:17)

Feet of Peace
(Ephesians 6:15)

NOTE:

The above scripture in verse 18 speaks about "pray in the Spirit". This has been referred to by many as speaking in tongues; however, the gift from the Holy Spirit of speaking in **tongues is not given to everyone**. This "pray in the Spirit" refers to "speaking the Word of God when you pray – repeating Scriptures according to what it is you are seeking Gods intervention for".

As seen next in 1 Corinthians 12:7-11, the Holy Spirit is the one who gives the different spiritual gifts **as He sees fit** for the benefit of all in the Body of Christ. They are not something we can "learn, buy or scheme to obtain". So then again, if Ephesians 6:18 says to "pray in the Spirit" **a highly recommended thing to do if you plan to have any chance of standing against Satan and his followers,** and 1 Corinthians 12:10 states only some receive the gift of speaking in various tongues (languages), praying the Scriptures is something **everyone** can do regardless of which spiritual gift(s) the Holy Spirit has given them.

The receiving of these spiritual gifts occur after a person has accepted Jesus Christ as their Lord and Savior, then they are spiritually baptized in the Holy Spirit, who comes and lives inside them. He is the comforter/helper Jesus spoke of who would replace Him when He ascended to Heaven after He was crucified (John 14:25-29).

1 Corinthians 12:7-11 New King James Version (NKJV)
The Holy Spirit gives spiritual gifts for the benefit of everyone, not for individual "fame"

7. But the manifestation of the Spirit is given to each one for the profit of all:

8. for to one is given the word of wisdom through the Spirit, to another the word of knowledge through the same Spirit,

9. to another faith by the same Spirit, to another gifts of healings by the same[b] Spirit,

10. to another the working of miracles, to another prophecy, to another discerning of spirits, **to another different kinds of tongues**, to another the interpretation of tongues.

11. But one and the same Spirit works all these things, distributing to each one individually as He wills.

John 14:25-29 New King James Version (NKJV)
The Gift of His Peace

25. "These things I have spoken to you while being present with you.

26. But the Helper, the Holy Spirit, whom the Father will send in My name, He will teach you all things, and bring to your remembrance all things that I said to you.

27. Peace I leave with you, My peace I give to you; not as the world gives do I give to you. Let not your heart be troubled, neither let it be afraid.

28. You have heard Me say to you, 'I am going away and coming back to you.' If you loved Me, you would rejoice because I said,[a] 'I am going to the Father,' for My Father is greater than I.

29. "And now I have told you before it comes, that when it does come to pass, you may believe.

CHAPTER NINE

How the Word of God is a Weapon against Marine Spirits

Isaiah 27:1 King James Version (KJV)

The sword of God (Word of God)

27. In that day the Lord with his sore and great and strong sword shall punish leviathan the piercing serpent, even leviathan that crooked serpent; and he shall slay the dragon that is in the sea.

Ezekiel 29:3-5 King James Version (KJV)

The hook of God to drag out of the water of our bodies the marine spirit as fish cannot live outside of water

3. Speak, and say, Thus saith the Lord God; Behold, I am against thee, Pharaoh king of Egypt, the great dragon that lieth in the midst of his rivers, which hath said, My river is mine own, and I have made it for myself.

4. But I will put hooks in thy jaws, and I will cause the fish of thy rivers to stick unto thy scales, and I will bring thee up out of the midst of thy rivers, and all the fish of thy rivers shall stick unto thy scales.

5. And I will leave thee thrown into the wilderness, thee and all the fish of thy rivers: thou shalt fall upon the open fields; thou shalt not be brought together, nor gathered: I have given thee for meat to the beasts of the field and to the fowls of the heaven.

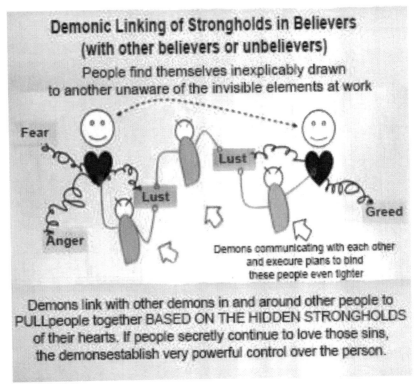

Demonic Linking of Strongholds in Believers (with other believers or unbelievers)

People find themselves inexplicably drawn to another unaware of the invisible elements at work

Fear
Lust
Lust
Greed
Anger

Demons communicating with each other and execute plans to bind these people even tighter

Demons link with other demons in and around other people to PULL people together BASED ON THE HIDDEN STRONGHOLDS of their hearts. If people secretly continue to love those sins, the demons establish very powerful control over the person.

Job 26:12-13 King James Version (KJV)

Ask for God to smite through the spirit of pride from the person, brought on by the spiritual spouse

12. He divideth the sea with his power, and by his understanding he smiteth through the proud.

13. By his spirit he hath garnished the heavens; his hand hath formed the crooked serpent.

The picture example is using spirit of lust. Like attracts like (perversion brings perversion, stealing brings stealing etc.)

1 Samuel 5:2-4 King James Version (KJV)

2. When the Philistines took the ark of God, they brought it into the house of Dagon, and set it by Dagon.

3. And when they of Ashdod arose early on the morrow, behold, Dagon was fallen upon his face to the earth before the ark of the Lord. And they took Dagon, and set him in his place again.

4. And when they arose early on the morrow morning, behold, Dagon was fallen upon his face to the ground before the ark of the Lord; and the head of Dagon and both the palms of his hands were cut off upon the threshold; only the stump of Dagon was left to him.

Revelation 12:11 King James Version (KJV)

Share your testimony to help others overcome

11. And they overcame him by the blood of the Lamb, and by the word of their testimony; and they loved not their lives unto the death.

2 Kings 2:19-21 King James Version (KJV)

Prophesy to the water

19. And the men of the city said unto Elisha, Behold, I pray thee, the situation of this city is pleasant, as my lord seeth: but the water is naught, and the ground barren.

20. And he said, Bring me a new cruse (bowl), and put salt therein. And they brought it to him.

21. And he went forth unto the spring of the waters, and cast the salt in there, and said, Thus saith the Lord, I have healed these waters; there shall not be from thence any more death or barren land.

Ezekiel 26:16-17 New King James Version (NKJV)

Prophesy to the water (marine spirits) for they will attack you at some point in your life

16. Then all the princes of the sea will come down from their thrones, lay aside their robes, and take off their embroidered garments; they will clothe themselves with trembling; they will sit on the ground, tremble every moment, and be astonished at you. 17 And they will take up a lamentation for you, and say to you:

"How you have perished,

O one inhabited by seafaring men,

O renowned city,

Who was strong at sea,

She and her inhabitants,

Who caused their terror to be on all her inhabitants!"

Ezekiel 27:27 New King James Version (NKJV)

This is what will happen to you after the marine spirits have attacked; they want to utterly destroy you

27. "Your riches, wares, and merchandise,

Your mariners and pilots,

Your caulkers and merchandisers,

All your men of war who are in you,

And the entire company which is in your midst,

Will fall into the midst of the seas on the day of your ruin.

Mark 5:12-13 New King James Version (NKJV)

The 2,000 spirits ended up in the water; demons are manipulative!

11. So all the demons begged Him, saying, "Send us to the swine, that we may enter them." 13. And at once Jesus[a] gave them permission. Then the unclean spirits went out and entered the swine (there were about two thousand); and the herd ran violently down the steep place into the sea, and drowned in the sea.

Beloved do not believe every spirit, but test the spirits to see whether thy are from God...

1 John 4:1

CHAPTER TEN

Night Visitors

Many people have suffered terrible problems and received the greatest attacks at night. A lot who were healthy, happy, with sound minds, went to sleep only to wake up with some mysterious sickness, mental disorder, business failure, death of a loved one, collapse of marriage and other problems due to a Night Visitor.

Matthew 13:25 New King James Version (NKJV)

25. but while men slept, his enemy came and sowed tares (they look like wheat but are not) among the wheat and went his way.

Sleep is a strong weapon of Satan. He has specialized in using the needed sleep of man as a form of anesthesia to carry out evil operations on them. Satan uses darkness to cover the attacks of his victims. The fact is that when a person falls asleep, they are extremely vulnerable to spiritual attacks.

Psalm 74:20 New King James Version (NKJV)
Respect Gods Word

20. Have respect to the covenant; For the dark places of the earth are full of the haunts of cruelty.

Every community in the earth has dark places. The communities in which we live are filled with invisible powers often using human agents, whose job is to wait for the dark hours and attack men, women, and children. For someone to be a member of that dark society they must be wicked; defiled by evil.

Job 4:12-14 New King James Version (NKJV)
Job's encounter with a night spirit

12. "Now a word was secretly brought to me, And my ear received a whisper of it.

13. In disquieting thoughts from the visions of the night, When deep sleep falls on men,

14. Fear came upon me, and trembling, Which made all my bones shake.

15. Then a spirit passed before my face; The hair on my body stood up.

16. It stood still, But I could not discern its appearance. A form was before my eyes;

Job was attacked by a night visitor. He did not anticipate for what happened to him. All Job wanted was to sleep but instead he woke up trembling and fearful as the dream was so vivid and real. This is because a spirit had visited him and placed the spirit of fear upon him. The spirit of fear gripped him so tightly that Job's hair stood on edge, embarrassing him. As a result of not rebuking the covenant forged in the dream with the evil spirit, Job's fears manifested in his life, evident from the loss of all he had. He lost his children, wealth and health to the edge of death. However, God allowed this to prove to Satan the deep level of Job's faith in his Heavenly Father.

Again, it is vital that you not only rebuke/come against any covenants in your dreams with Satan, BUT also come into agreement with those in your dreams that are with God. Having God's will play out in our lives will ensure we are restored if not in this life, in eternity with all the blessings God has for us.

Now even though Job didn't come against the covenant in his dream with Satan, the test was as a result of an agreement between God and Satan. In essence Satan told God he could make Job curse Him if God would remove the spiritual hedge (wall) of protection from around Job and all that was his. God in His infinite wisdom, knowing the heart of Job as He does ALL humans, agreed to remove His protection off of Job. The one condition was that Satan could not take Jobs life.

After Satan tried his best to get Job to curse God and failed, God restored Job to a place of having more than he did before the tests and trials of Satan came into his life. So you may wonder "well how is that possible?" It is possible because Job had previously made a covenant with God; Job obeyed the commandments of God and trusted all that he was and had to God. In a nutshell, when we honor God, He will honor and keep us through all the trials of life.

For us today, after the blood sacrifice Jesus Christ made on the cross at Calvary, where his death and resurrection did away with the laws that Job followed, we are now only covered/protected by making a covenant with Jesus Christ to have Him as our Lord and Savior. It is the only way to salvation and access to God, as the animal sacrifices that man used to offer up to God could no longer atone for the sin and vileness that was upon the earth.

John 14:6 New International Version (NIV)

7. Jesus answered, "I am the way and the truth and the life. No one comes to the Father except through me.

John 5:20-30 New International Version (NIV)

20. For the Father loves the Son and shows him all he does. Yes, and he will show him even greater works than these, so that you will be amazed.

21. For just as the Father raises the dead and gives them life, even so the Son gives life to whom he is pleased to give it.

22. Moreover, the Father judges no one, but has entrusted all judgment to the Son,

23. that all may honor the Son just as they honor the Father. Whoever does not honor the Son does not honor the Father, who sent him.

24. "Very truly I tell you, whoever hears my word and believes him who sent me has eternal life and will not be judged but has crossed over from death to life.

25. Very truly I tell you, a time is coming and has now come when the dead will hear the voice of the Son of God and those who hear will live.

26. For as the Father has life in himself, so he has granted the Son also to have life in himself.

27. And he has given him authority to judge because he is the Son of Man.

28. "Do not be amazed at this, for a time is coming when all who are in their graves will hear his voice

29. and come out—those who have done what is good will rise to live, and those who have done what is evil will rise to be condemned.

30. By myself I can do nothing; I judge only as I hear, and my judgment is just, for I seek not to please myself but him who sent me.

Ephesians 5:11 New King James Version (NKJV)

11. And have no fellowship with the unfruitful works of darkness (sin), but rather expose them.

Satanic night raiders have destroyed many lives. All of the physical steps taken to protect you and your property from thieves cannot assist you in the Spirit Realm. Spirits don't use the doors or windows of buildings to get access to you. They are constantly carrying out their assignments.

Why Night Visitors Come at Night

- Darkness is the absence of light
- Darkness is not a positive creation
- Darkness is the result of obscuring light
- People find darkness uncomfortable because of uncertainty
- Darkness can cause a person to lose his way
- Darkness can make a person wander
- Darkness can make a person expose him/her to danger
- Darkness can make a person stumble (you can't see where you are going)

Jeremiah 13:16 New King James Version (NKJV)

If the "darkness" is allowed by God, you need to address the sin in your life in order to be delivered from the darkness

16. Give glory to the Lord your God, Before He causes darkness, And before your feet stumble, On the dark mountains, And while you are looking for light, He turns it into the shadow of death, And makes it dense darkness.

There are degrees of darkness; partial, medium, and complete. For example if you try to cast light in a large room with only a candle, you will see that most of the light will be near the candle. The further away you look from the candle, the darker the space appears. God's Word says we should so let our light shine from within us. Darkness is silent; it has binding and separating power.

Matthew 5:14-18 New King James Version (NKJV)

14. "You are the light of the world. A city that is set on a hill cannot be hidden.

15 . Nor do they light a lamp and put it under a basket, but on a lampstand, and it gives light to all who are in the house.

16. Let your light so shine before men, that they may see your good works and glorify your Father in heaven.

Satan has released upon men, an army of night visitors. The night is most conductive for evil activity by the spirits, who carry out their assignments. Some of what is conducted through men who have made covenants (known and unknown) with these evil spirits are:

- Sacrifices
- Robbery
- Witchcraft attacks
- Demonic meetings/gatherings
- Parties/clubs/ bars (places used to get people to let down their guard through music, alcohol, drugs, lust etc.)
- Drug houses

Who are Night Visitors?

- **Marine Powers** - whose main job is to get man to be disobedient to God's commandment to love Him above all else, and to get man to trust in the demonic powers in order to gain control, riches, territory, and ruler-ship over others.

- **Familiar Spirits** - these go about confusing man, causing disaster, ruining lives. Their power is the knowledge they have of their targets, since they have been assigned to watch them from birth, recording everything about them only to use it against them later in life.

- *They also love when people keep secrets instead of confessing them and being free.*

- **Witchcraft Powers** - these are well known even if not confessed by many in the world. Though witches and warlocks are active during the day, most of what they do is done under the dark cover of night. While people are going to sleep, witchcraft powers start to send attacks to destroy their lives most often from evil altars.

- **Forest Demons** - these will sometimes move out of their domain and join with people, bringing fear and a sense of being lost. For people who have dreams where they are getting lost in a forest, this type of spirit is active in their life *(such as Boraro of South America, those in the Aokigahara Forest of Japan, Hoia-Baciu Forest of Transylvania).*

- **Wandering Spirits** - they do as their name suggests, wander about looking for human bodies to possess. Many in the world think of them as the lost souls of the dead, who are trapped in purgatory, however, these are evil spirits following out their assignments. This also exposes the idea of reincarnation...

Ecclesiastes 9:5-6 New International Version (NIV)

5. For the living know that they will die, but the dead know nothing; they have no further   reward, and even their name is forgotten.
6. Their love, their hate and their jealousy have long since vanished; never again will they have a part in anything that happens under the sun.

- **Evil Angels** - these powers have the ability to look like a normal person, who will disappear if their true identity is found out. An example would be if you see someone off in the distance and something about them seems peculiar in your spirit. Only to look away for a brief moment, in which time they disappear. This would be opposite yet similar to the below scripture as Satan built his strategy as the opposite of God's Word:

Hebrews 13:2 King James Version (KJV)

2. Be not forgetful to entertain strangers: for thereby some have entertained angels unawares.

- **Wicked Personalities** - these display in people who do wicked against others for their own personal gain. They control and manipulate their victims to continuously seek out self-fulfillment, which is only keeping the covenant active; bondage.

- **Occult Powers** - such as secret societies (Freemasons, Lodges, Fraternities, Sororities), also any non-secret club making oaths and pledges unto any other spirit than God.

- **Recruitment Agents** - these seek out people with any level of evil in them to initiate them into deeper spiritual bondage. These can also approach and observe people through their control of humans.

- **Spirits Impersonating the Dead** - these you see as someone who is dead either while awake (a brief glimpse) or in a dream. Their goal is to make you comfortable or at ease allowing them to trick /manipulate or initiate you into spiritual bondage with little or no resistance from you.

- **Satanic Spies** - regardless what you think, the Spirit Realm has levels of agents that collect all sorts of information on man; reconnaissance. These do not necessarily have to be spirits; many humans allow themselves through covenants of some type of "false gains" to be used for the collection of intelligence on other people.

- **Dream Manipulators** - just as God uses dreams to communicate with man, so does Satan and his followers. These manipulate your dreams into seemingly harmless things or nonsense, only to create covenants with you, which you DO NOT rebuke upon waking because you think your dreams are meaningless. You must rebuke dreams from Satan.

Some Attributes of Night Visitors

- They eat away at the flesh of their victims and drink their blood in the form of sickness and disease.
- They entice their victims with food in their dreams, trying to get them to ingest the foods which are really curses in disguise.
- Will take on the form of an idol in the victim's life; something they cherish, a person, thing or activity.
- They go after everyone in the home through at least one person, who becomes the gateway for other spirits to

take up ownership of the property. You would have to spiritually cleanse the property to get rid of them.

- They **are** the spirits of death and hell.

Luke 22:53 New King James Version (NKJV)
When they came to arrest Jesus before His crucifixion

52. Then Jesus said to the chief priests, captains of the temple, and the elders who had come to Him, "Have you come out, as against a robber, with swords and clubs?

53. When I was with you daily in the temple, you did not try to seize Me. But this is your hour, and the power of darkness."

The above scripture shows that Jesus admits that darkness has its own power.

Why Night Visitors Succeed

- Sin in people's lives that have not been repented of.
- Curses that remain in place and have not been broken by the intended person or another in their family for deliverance of the entire bloodline.
- Evil covenants knowingly or unknowingly made by that person or someone dead or alive in their family.

- Lack of deliverance in the person's life. It could be partial deliverance from sin, with some unaddressed sin still remaining.
- Bad spiritual environment such as a broken home, home full of unbelievers, evil at work on a job etc.
- Backsliding has occurred in a person's life, meaning they do not follow the ways of Jesus Christ 100%. Want to have one foot still in the "world".

Psalm 130 New King James Version (NKJV)
For the backslider *(a person who is following Christ but doesn't really understand Gods Word even though they want to – through their weakness in God, sin keeps pulling then back to parts of their old life)*

Waiting for the Redemption of the LORD - A Song of Ascents.

1. Out of the depths I have cried to You, O Lord;
2. Lord, hear my voice! Let Your ears be attentive. To the voice of my supplications.

3. If You, Lord, should mark iniquities, O Lord, who could stand?
4. But there is forgiveness with You, That You may be feared.

5. I wait for the Lord, my soul waits, And in His word I do hope.

6. My soul waits for the Lord, More than those who watch for the morning— Yes, more than those who watch for the morning.

7. O Israel, hope in the Lord; For with the Lord there is mercy, And with Him is abundant redemption.
8. And He shall redeem Israel, From all his iniquities.

CHAPTER ELEVEN

Identifying Spirits in Me

You can use the following questionnaire to better understand the spirit(s) at work in your life. Once you have this knowledge, you can then use the Word of God to free yourself and family from them.

Your overall score is calculated by taking your Score Sum divided by 30. For example if you add up the score number for each of the 30 questions and get 91, you would then calculate 91/30 = 3.03 the higher your score, the more evident you are dealing with an evil spirit in your life.

For statements you have a score of 3, 4 or 5, these are the areas that Satan and his spirits are successfully attacking you in - you need deliverance in these areas. Statements with a score of 1 or 2 are not areas of Satan's main attacks; however, you should get deliverance from these areas also.

Instructions - read each statement and score it based on your life as:

1 = Never   4 = Often

2 = Seldom   5 = A lot

3 = Usually

Questionnaire:

1 I do not pray for sanctification over the food I eat or liquids I drink.

2 I often have dreams of water.

3 I live in an area with a lot of natural water sources (ocean, rivers, lakes, streams).

4 I have idols in my life (things/people I adore, cherish, am a "fan" of).

5 I serve The Most High God _and_ other gods (pledges in Greek organizations, Secret Societies, etc.).

6 I have sexual dreams.

7 Find that a lot of my personal belongings simply disappear.

8 I have been involved in Satanism or witchcraft (either of my own will or that of family heritage).

9 I have practiced astral projection/traveling.

10 I have visited one of the Marine Kingdoms in the rivers, lakes, streams or oceans (physically and/or in dreams).

11 I have asked for supernatural power from sources other than The Most High God.

12 I have acquired riches from spiritual sources other than The Most High God.

13 I have acquired and operated in powers received from sources other than The Most High God.

14 I have exercised divination (fortune telling, divining, soothsaying, augury, clairvoyance, second sight etc.).

15 I have performed incantations (summoning the dead, trying to talk to the dead or spirits).

16 I have tossed coins into ponds, fountains, wishing wells and made a wish.

17 I have visited herbalists/witchdoctors for power or protection (not herbalists for medicinal herbs).

18 I find myself wanting power to rule over others.

19 I possess magical powers.

20 I visited occultist to rid me of spiritual entities.

21 I draw from spiritual entities to attain success.

22 I performed rituals to have others love me
    (love spells, love potions).

23 I gave others portions to consume to control
    their emotions (other than love, to make them
    make choices that I wanted them to make;
    take away their free will).

24 I dream of swimming.

25 I dream of drowning.

26 Cults and other religions are abundant in the
    area I live.

27 I/My spouse/ My parents have suffered a
    sudden miscarriage during pregnancy.

28 The political or spiritual rulers in my country
    are guilty of immorality.

29 I have been divorced.

30 I approve of public nudity.

Overcoming Spirits in Your Life

- Give your life to The Most High God, ask Jesus Christ to be your Lord and Savior - this is **non-negotiable**, without doing this, nothing else will help you be free.

- Repent from all inherited and personal sins.

- Break every soul tie with all spirit spouses.

- Pray aggressively against their activities in your life. Burn spiritual marriage rings, certificates, wedding garments, children etc. with Holy Ghost Fire through prayer.

- Get deliverance (self-deliverance prayer at end of book if you need it)

- Receive the baptism of the Holy Ghost through prayer.

- Determine to live holy.

- Make reading God's Word a frequent and daily practice in your life.

- Add fasting to your faith walk. Ask God to direct you on how often, when, length and type of fasts to take.

- Pray and let God direct you as to how you can help others in ministry for Him.

CHAPTER TWELVE

How Can I Be Set Free?

From a spirit spouse:

1. Repent of any known and unknown sin in your life (understand this is an intensive processes - some specific areas you can speak against that you've participated in are listed below).

Promiscuity	Juvenile Delinquency	Immorality	Death
Enchantments	Witchcraft	Caging of Souls	Doubt
Idolatry	Multiple Marriages/ Divorce	Disobedience/ Rebellion	Sorceries
Seducing Others	Antichrist	Persecuting Others (no man is sinless)	Bloodshed
Insanity	Infertility	Ungodly Marriages (via coercion)	Deceiving Others
Infirmities (sickness)	Sexual Immorality (sex other than with opposite gender, with animals, with objects)	Following False Spirit Guides	Murder
Prostitution (sex for anything)	Self-worship (Narcissism)	Poverty	

2. Ask God to help you to fully forgive those that have done evil to you. Also, forgive yourself for the destructive choices you've made in the past.

3. Identify if possible, the door through which you got the spirit husband or wife. Fast and pray asking God to show you where you got it if uncertain. Once you know, call it out by name.

    a. If it was through sexual sin, call out the name of the person(s) that you know where the point of contact. If you don't remember the names ask God to reveal them to you.

    b. Sinful emotions you have kept in your heart should also be included in your repentant prayer such as:

Fear	Stress	Anxiety
Lust	Insecurity	Anger
Greed	Deep Hurt	Rejection
Abandonment	Fear of Death	Fear of Drowning
Fear of Rejection	Fear of the Ocean or Water	Excessive Fear of Rivers
Hatred	Sorrow	Self-rejection
Pride	Hopelessness	

4. Destroy any gifts from the relationship which the spirit spouse used to gain access to you. All things from your ex-boyfriend or ex-girlfriend destroy with fire if you can or throw away. There may be some things you can keep – **pray and confirm with God first on these items.**

5. Daily plead the <u>redemptive power of the Blood of Jesus over yourself</u>.

> ***Pray:*** " Father God by the victorious and redemptive power of the Blood of Jesus, break the sole ties, detach me from this spirit spouse brought to me through the relationship I had with _____. In the name of Jesus and the power of His Blood, break the covenant Father in Jesus name I pray."

Prayer for Deliverance

6. Pray these scripture references **to deliver yourself and renounce** the spiritual marriage **and** the following prayer:

Matthew 22:30 ... After death there is no marriage. Spirits are not supposed to marry.

Leviticus 19:19 ...even cattle are not supposed to sleep with any other animal but cattle; which presupposes that human beings do not sleep with spirits and so I divorce every spirit in Jesus' name.

2 Corinthians 11:2 -- this scripture admonishes that I am married to Jesus so every spirit husband or wife is divorced in the name of Jesus.

Deuteronomy 24:1-4 – I issue a certificate of divorce against the spirit husband or wife.

Colossians 2:14 --Blotts out the handwriting of ordinances that was against us, which was contrary to us, and took it out of the way, nailing it to His cross.

(Note: parts of prayer below that apply to marriages still repeat even if not married to prevent future issues)

In the precious and mighty name of Jesus:

- ❖ I renounce every marital vow or agreements entered into by my ancestors or my immediate parents on my behalf, now or before my birth.

- ❖ I break and deactivate all vows or covenants entered into with a spirit spouse.

- ❖ By faith, I withdraw every engagement material, visible or invisible, presented to the Spirit World on my behalf.

- ❖ I command the fire of God to burn to ashes the spiritual wedding attire, rings, photographs, marriage certificate and all other materials used for the wedding.

- ❖ I break every demonic blood covenant as a result of having sex, food, or ceremonies in my dream with a spirit spouse.

- ❖ Let all demonic children which I have had (consciously or unconsciously) in the Spirit Realm, be consumed by fire.

- ❖ By the power in the Blood of Jesus and under His new covenant, I withdraw my DNA, my blood, my destiny and any other part of my body deposited on the altar of a spirit spouse.

- ❖ I receive spiritual authority to break all marital vows and covenants, and to affect an everlasting divorce between the spirit spouse and myself, in the name of the Father, the Son and the Holy Spirit.

- ❖ I call on heaven and earth to witness this day that I return all demonic properties in my possession back to the Spirit World, including symbols, dowry, and whatsoever was presented on the satanic altar or shrine for the marriage ceremony.

- ❖ Let the Blood of Jesus purge my system of all wrongful sex and all demonic deposits.

- Let the flood light of the Holy Spirit, search my body and expose and destroy every demonic mark, tag, or exclusion deposited in my life.

- I command every strange image, object, or symbol deposited by the spirit spouse to come out of my life.

- I break the head of the snake; deposited into my body by the spirit spouse to do me harm, and command it to come out.

- I send my body to the heavenly surgical room for a complete operation to repair, restore, or put right any damage done to any part of my body and/or my earthly marriage, by the spirit spouse.

- I reject and renounce the demonic name given to me by the spirit spouse and I soak myself in the Blood of Jesus and cancel every demonic mark attached to such names.

- I request the Judge of Heaven and Earth to issue a standing decree order of restriction to every spirit spouse harassing me in my dreams.

- I destroy every demonic power assigned to destabilize my earthly marriage and ability to bear children.

- May the Lord Jesus Christ rebuke every demonic agent commissioned from the spirit spouse to cause misunderstanding between my spouse and I.

❖ With immediate effect, I abandon and disown any spiritual children attached to my name from the spirit spouse and ask my Heavenly Father to do with them as He sees fit.

I plead the blood of Jesus Christ over me and my family. Thank you Heavenly Father for your grace and mercy in Jesus name I pray, amen.

A Prayer Cancelling and Coming into Agreement

(with things in your dreams and to be able to recall forgotten dreams):

"Father I know I just had a dream, but I don't remember anything of it.

I cancel everything of that dream that is not of you.

Father I cancel it, I reject it, I renounce it, I disassociate myself with all the powers of the Kingdom of Darkness that are related to that dream.

Any evil covenants that would have been subtly forged in that dream, I disassociate myself,

I cancel, I reject, I renounce, I cancel all agreements period that are not with you Father.

It shall not take shape in my life, the life of my family members and anyone that dream's pertaining to.

However, if the dream is of you Father God, then I bind myself to what you desire for my life.

Because according to your Word in Jeremiah 29:11 it says your thoughts towards me are good and not evil and that I will have an expected end.

Therefore, I can trust you that if the dream is from you then it is something to benefit me.

Reveal to me what that is and I come wholeheartedly in agreement with it,

in Jesus name I pray, amen."

Shorter Version- Cancelling/Agreement

"Heavenly Father I **come into** agreement
with any covenant made in my dream that
was with you and,

I **come against** any covenant in my dream
made with Satan.

Please reveal to me what you want me to
know about my dream,

in Jesus name I pray, amen."

A Prayer Asking God to Reveal to You Things About People and Situations

"Father God you know all things, nothing is hidden from you as your Word says in Psalms 139.

Your Word declares that whatever is spoken *(done)* in the dark shall surely come to light as in Luke 12:3.

Reveal to me your servant what is being hidden from me.

Father even if you have to show it to me in a dream, reveal to me the things I cannot see physically.

Show your servant in the realm of the spirit what is being orchestrated in terms of keeping things from me that I would be ignorant to it.

Reveal the trap to me, in Jesus name I pray, amen."

A Prayer to Help You Be Able to Focus on What God is Showing You in Dreams

"Father God, clearly there is something on the horizon for me. Settle my spirit; remove the anger, bitterness, being argumentative, all of those things that are hindering me from focusing on the real issue. Now Lord, condition me to focus on the Spiritual Realm.

Now I curse the spirit of confusion, I curse and bind the spirits of frustration and anger, and I come against every force that is trying to pull me away from focusing on the Laws of God, which says in 2 Corinthians 4:18 that I must not focus on what I see, but pay attention to the unseen world.

Father God, I refuse to fight flesh and blood of my boss, mother, father, supervisor, pastor, minister; whoever is coming up against me Lord.

Father take resentment from me, because that is the first thing that Satan is trying to inject into me to build up a wall against them.
Instead Lord, let me flow in your Word.
I reject bitterness; I reject un-forgiveness; I forgive those that come against me Lord.

Now Lord, cause me to be realigned with the journey you had originally placed me on, to welcome, to interact, to align with the things that you have prepared for me **THIS DAY** and in days to come, in Jesus name, amen."

ABOUT THE AUTHOR

"First **THANK YOU** for supporting my work
and **please leave a review** on the website you
purchased it from…..
reviews are life!"

Zita Grant is a freelance writer, author, computer coding tech-head, avid reader, self-proclaimed movie critic and social media buff. Yet of the things she does, learning and sharing the wonderful "Good New of Jesus Christ" tops them all.

Some of her other passions include cooking, food tasting, gardening and traveling. Whenever she's not busy writing novels, debugging some computer language code, or helping coach other writers, her time is spent enjoying the outdoors with friends and family….or making a larger dent in her sofa watching a movie (80% of the time it would be a Foreign Film).

Keep up to date with Zita's latest offerings and events by connecting on:

FaceBook

Instagram

Twitter

All with User Name @ZitaG_Author

REFERENCES

Zondervan. "BibleGateway." *BibleGateway.com: A Searchable Online Bible in over 150 Versions and 50 Languages.*, Zondervan, 1 Jan. 2008, *www.biblegateway.com/.*

(1a) *Borgmann, Albert (2006). "Technology as a Cultural Force: For Alena and Griffin" (fee required). The Canadian Journal of Sociology. **31** (3): 351–60. doi:10.1353/cjs.2006.0050. Retrieved 3 October 2017.*

Amoah-Boateng, Reverand Seth. "How to Divorce from a Spirit Husband or Spirit Wife." *YouTube*, YouTube, 28 May 2014, www.youtube.com/watch?v=YO88H7uTeaE. Accessed 28 Sept. 2017.

Olukoya, Dr. D. K. *Deliverance from Spirit Husband and Spirit Wife.* 2nd ed., Nigeria, The Battle Cry Christian Ministries, 2001.

Kee, H. C. (1994). *The NRSV Cambridge Annotated Study Apocrypha* (1st ed.). New York, NY: Cambridge University Press.

Solomon, Reverand James A. *Deliverance from Demonic Covenants & Curses.* 2nd ed., Norcross, GA, Jesus People Publication, 2007.

Kwekudee. "TRIP DOWN MEMORY LANE." *MAMI WATA: THE SACRED FEMALE AFRICAN WATER DEITY*, Blogger, 19 Dec. 2012, kwekudee-tripdownmemorylane.blogspot.com/2012/12/mami-wata-sacred-female-african-water_19.html. Accessed 29 Sept. 2017.

King, E. (2011, November 07). Power Against Spiritual Marriages - Part 1. Retrieved September 30, 2017, from https://www.youtube.com/watch?v=jWkL_wcJ6cY

Ewing, Minister K. L. (1970, January 01). Journey Into God's Word. Retrieved September 28, 2017, from http://kevinlaewing.blogspot.com/

C. (2015, August 03). Indian Hair Sacrifice -Wear The Weave Comes From. Retrieved October 02, 2017, from https://www.youtube.com/watch?v=l74nwgSyqYE

J. (2016, July 06). The Hair-Brained Fashion Scheme Making Billions of Dollars. Retrieved October 02, 2017, from https://www.youtube.com/watch?v=M2lvzmkWbao

Made in the USA
Middletown, DE
31 October 2017